KU-373-811

HAROLD ROSENTHAL

COVENT GARDEN

Memories and Traditions

Folio Miniatures

MICHAEL JOSEPH

LONDON

FOLIO MINIATURES
General Editor : John Letts

KING ALFRED'S COLLEGE
WINCHESTER

782·1
ROS
46112

First published in Great Britain by
Michael Joseph Ltd
52 Bedford Square
London WC1B 3EF
1976

© 1976 Harold Rosenthal

All Rights Reserved. No part of this publication may
be reproduced, stored in a retrieval system, or
transmitted in any form or by any means, electronic,
mechanical, photocopying, recording or otherwise,
without the prior permission of the Copyright
owner

ISBN 0 7181 1474 4

*The endpaper shows a picture of the Floral Hall and the
Royal Opera House, Covent Garden, c. 1861 :* by courtesy of
the Victoria and Albert Museum.

PRINTED AND BOUND IN BELGIUM
by Henri Proost & Cie p.v.b.a., Turnhout

THE EARLY DAYS

To many people the name Covent Garden has always conjured up the fruit and vegetable market, which after more than 300 years has only recently, in 1975, moved from the Covent Garden area; to the opera and ballet lover, however, and to the practitioners of those two arts the world over, Covent Garden means the Royal Opera House in London. Indeed, there has been a Covent Garden Theatre on roughly the same site as the present one since 1732; and although it only became an opera house in 1847, its links with musical entertainment of one kind or another go back to 1732, when the first Covent Garden Theatre – there have been three on the same site – opened its doors.

This first Covent Garden Theatre was built by John Rich, the producer and actor, who had in his possession 'Letters Patent', originally granted by King Charles II to the famous actor Sir William Davenant. This patent empowered the holder to erect a theatre 'within our cities of London and Westminster or the suburbs thereof'. Rich had already built his first theatre in Lincoln's Inn Fields in 1714, and there, in collaboration with the poet and playright John Gay, and the composer Pepusch, produced the famous *Beggar's Opera* in 1728. So successful did this prove – the wags of the day said it 'made Rich gay and Gay rich' – that Rich looked round for a suitable site on which to build a second. He was able to obtain the lease of a piece of land that was 'contiguous to Bow Street, Hart Street, and Covent Garden' and which belonged, as did most of the area, to the Duke of Bedford. This land had once been the property of the Catholic Church; in fact, it had been a *convent* garden – which, in course of time, became known as Covent Garden.

3

When Henry VIII dissolved the monasteries, he had given this land to the Russell family – John Russell became the Earl of Bedford in 1550. Even today, there is a private box in the Opera House known as the Bedford Box; it is never put on sale to the public and it has its own private entrance from Floral Street, which runs the length of the theatre on its north side. The theatre had been built by virtue of Rich's possessing a royal patent so it was allowed to be the Theatre *Royal*, Covent Garden, and eventually the Royal Opera House.

Rich opened the theatre on 7th December, 1732 with a performance of Congreve's *The Way of the World*; the first musical piece to be heard there was, not unnaturally, *The Beggar's Opera*, which followed as the second performance. The life of the first Covent Garden Theatre, however, was not primarily an operatic one; it was the home of drama, sharing with the other Theatre Royal, that at Drury Lane, the great names of the British stage – Garrick and Peg Woffington, the Kembles and Mrs Siddons, Macready and Kean. There was, however, one glorious operatic interlude in the 1730s and 1740s, when Handel became closely associated with Covent Garden, following his withdrawal from the King's Theatre in the Haymarket after his quarrel with the castrato, Senesino, in 1735.

In addition to the performance of ballad opera at Covent Garden in the second half of the 18th century, there were two short seasons of Italian opera there in 1789 and 1790: these owed nothing to any particular enterprise on the part of the theatre's management, but rather to the fire that had destroyed the King's Theatre in June 1789. The company of the King's Theatre included the famous soprano, Ann Storace, who had created Susanna in Mozart's *Le nozze di Figaro* in Vienna three years earlier; the Irish tenor, Michael Kelly, who had been the first Don Basilio and Don Curzio in the same opera; and the Italian bass, Francesco Benucci, the original Figaro, and first Guglielmo in *Così fan tutte*. After that, little real opera was heard in the first Covent Garden Theatre; and on 19th September, 1808, it caught fire and was burned to the ground overnight.

4

THE SECOND THEATRE

Three months after the fire, on 30th December, 1808, the Prince of Wales laid the foundation stone of the second theatre; it weighed three tons (and can still be seen in the north-east corner of the basement of the present theatre). The new building was completed in less than a year. This theatre was designed by Richard Smirke, better remembered as the architect of the British Museum, the Mint and the General Post Office, and was said to be the largest theatre in Europe. The front was modelled partly on the Temple of Minerva at Athens, and the four fluted columns, which separated the portico, were said to be almost as large as those of St Peter's in Rome. The bas-reliefs on either side of the portico were designed by Flaxman and Rossi; they depicted classical and modern poets, and scenes from Shakespeare; surviving the second fire of 1856, they are now incorporated in the facade of the present Opera House, facing Bow Street Police Station.

The second theatre opened on 18th September, 1809, almost a year to the day after the destruction of the first. The opening night was a double bill, comprising Shakespeare's *Macbeth*, with Kemble and Mrs Siddons in the leading roles, and a 'Musical Entertainment, *The Quaker*'. Because of the vast expenditure in building, equipping and staffing the new theatre – more than £300,000 had been spent – the management decided to raise the prices of admission. Boxes were increased to seven shillings, and the pit to three shillings. This, coupled with the fact that the whole of the third tier was occupied by private boxes, gave rise to one of the most famous episodes in British theatrical history, the O.P. (Old Price) riots. The public believed that the increases had been made in order to engage foreign singers at exorbitant fees and, indeed, the management had engaged the famous soprano Catalani to sing in a series of concerts: she was probably the highest paid prima donna in

5

operatic history. Her salary in 1807 had amounted to £5,000 from her operatic appearances and £16,700 from her concerts; she is said to have been paid as much as two hundred guineas just to sing *God Save the King* and *Rule Britannia*.

And so the public rioted in the theatre. The opening night's *Macbeth* was all but inaudible, as every sound from the stage was 'drowned in a continued hissing, groaning, yelling, braying, barking, and hooting noises, accompanied by exclamations of "Old prices! No rise! No Catalani! No private boxes! No seven shilling pieces!"'. The demonstrations continued for all of two months and, finally, on 16th December, Kemble the elder, the famous actor who was also the theatre's manager, reduced the prices of the pit to 3/6d., and opened a number of the private boxes to the general public.

During the first part of the second theatre's life, various unrecognizable versions of Mozart's operas were given, generally with additional numbers by Henry Bishop, the theatre's musical director. In 1824 Charles Kemble, who had succeeded his father as manager, refused to pay Bishop an increase in salary. Bishop resigned in May of that year; and the following month Kemble invited Weber to become Covent Garden's musical director, and commissioned him to compose an opera for the theatre at a fee of £500.

Appropriately enough the 1825–6 season opened with Weber's *Der Freischütz*, which received fifty-three performances that season. Weber himself arrived in London on 5th March, 1826 and began to rehearse the opera he had written for Covent Garden, *Oberon*, with a libretto by Planché – 'a pigtrough of a libretto' was how the famous musicologist Donald Tovey described it almost a century later. The cast of the first performance included some of the finest British singers of the day: Ann Paton, Elizabeth Vestris and John Braham among them. Weber, already a dying man when he arrived in London, conducted; the settings and costumes were said to have surpassed 'everything of the kind seen before on the stage'. Weber's health declined, and on 5th June, thirteen weeks after his arrival in England, he died. A special performance of

*Carl Maria von Weber, the first foreign musical director of
Covent Garden* (Mansell Collection)

Oberon to help raise money for his widow and children was
given on 17th June. In all, there were thirty-two performances
of this opera, the most important work to be commissioned for
Covent Garden from a living composer until the 1950s.

From the death of Weber until the year Covent Garden
became the Royal Italian Opera in 1847, a period of just over
twenty years, there was a succession of managers at Covent
Garden, some good, some bad, and a few indifferent. They
included names well-known in London's theatrical and operatic
history: Charles Kemble, Laporte, Bunn, and Mme Vestris.
Each was responsible for at least one important operatic event

at Covent Garden before it became an official opera house. Thus Kemble brought the legendary Maria Malibran to Covent Garden for the first time in 1830 (she had already been appearing at the King's Theatre); Laporte put on a confection during Lent of 1833, which was made up of Rossini's *Mosè*, with additional music from Handel's *The Israelites in Egypt* and given with 'scenery and action' – it apparently 'drew the town'; in May of the same year, Bunn brought a German opera company to Covent Garden, whose star attraction was the soprano, Wilhemine Schröder-Devrient (known as the 'Queen of Tears', she was the singer who inspired Wagner to become an operatic composer) and Mme Vestris established a strong British operatic company, whose leading singers were Adelaide Kemble, Charles Kemble's daughter and younger sister of the actress and diarist, and Mary Shaw, who had sung in Verdi's first opera, *Oberto*, and other works at La Scala, Milan.

At one time or another during these various seasons a number of famous singers including Grisi, Tamburini, Zegler, and the conductor Costa made fleeting appearances on the stage of the theatre that was to become their home from 1847 when Covent Garden became the Royal Italian Opera.

AN OPERA HOUSE AT LAST

The events that led to the establishment of a second Italian Opera House in London (the King's Theatre in the Haymarket, known as Her Majesty's after the accession of Queen Victoria, had long been the leading Italian opera house in the capital) are too complicated to discuss fully in a short history. Briefly, Her Majesty's Royal Italian Opera in the Haymarket, under the musical direction of Michael Costa, and with a company that included great names like Pasta, Grisi, Persiani, Rubini, Donzelli, Mario, Tamburini, and Lablache, gave splendid seasons of opera each year from March until August.

'Her Majesty's State-Box at the Royal Italian Opera, Covent Garden'
from an Illustrated London News of 1848

The manager of the theatre, Benjamin Lumley, refused to submit to the various demands imposed on him by a powerful cabal of artists, known as 'La Vieille Garde', and an equally powerful group of subscribers, members of the nobility and gentry, who provided the necessary financial support for the season. The singers, led by the soprano Giulia Grisi, tried to influence Lumley in the choice of repertory and of new singers.

Following a refusal by Lumley to allow his musical director Costa to assume a similar position with the Philharmonic Society, and his demand (rather than request) that an opera from his own pen should be mounted every other year, Costa resigned. He was succeeded by the composer Balfe – not the strongest of musical directors. Meanwhile there were frequent replacements of leading singers, especially of Mario and Grisi, who were continually announcing they were 'indisposed' and unable to appear. So the affairs of Lumley and Her Majesty's went from bad to worse.

It was Charles Gruneissen, influential music critic of the *Morning Chronicle*, the music publisher Frederick Beale, the composer Giuseppe Persiani (whose wife Fanny Persiani had created Donizetti's *Lucia di Lammermoor* and was a member of Lumley's company) and the ousted Costa who were the leaders of the movement to establish a second Italian Opera in London. By chance the lease of Covent Garden was available, and with Beale as manager and director of the new undertaking, it was decided to change Covent Garden from a theatre into an opera house. The necessary architectural changes were drawn up by the architect Benedict Albano, who obtained possession of the theatre in December 1846. On 6th April, 1847, the new Royal Italian Opera, Covent Garden was ready to open with a performance of Rossini's *Semiramide*.

Opera has never been really economically viable, and the first season of Covent Garden's new life as a fully fledged opera house lost £24,000; the second and third under the management of the wealthy amateur, Edward Delafield, £34,756 and £25,455, which took him to the bankruptcy court. His successor was Frederick Gye, who took over in 1850 and whose regime

The Grand Staircase on the re-opening night of Covent Garden, from an Illustrated London News *of April 1847*

lasted until 1877, when he was succeeded by his son Frederick. Gye was the son of a tea and wine merchant who had a pecuniary interest in the theatre in that he provided the oil, soap, and candles for the dressing rooms and other parts of the building. He was a good business man, and turned the loss of the previous seasons into a profit of £4,226; he paid himself a salary of £1,500 as 'sole director and manager'.

In a way, Gye was the model of an operatic impresario; he successfully enlisted the support of Queen Victoria and the Prince Consort; he was enough of a diplomat to listen to suggestions made by his leading singers and his musical director Costa; and often gave the impression that he was acting on their advice when, in fact, what he was really doing was carrying out his own ideas. He was careful never to cross his leading sopranos Grisi and (later) Patti, and at times acceded to some of their more reasonable requests! It was not until 1869 when he temporarily joined forces with his old rival, Mapleson, manager of the rival Royal Italian Opera in London, that he came into a head on clash with Costa over musical and artistic matters. But it was Costa and not Gye who left Covent Garden.

Between 1848 and 1856, the year the second Covent Garden Theatre was destroyed by fire during a Bal Masqué, the first performances in England of *Rigoletto*, *Il trovatore*, *Le Prophète*, and *Benvenuto Cellini* took place. It is amusing and salutary to read what the critics of the day thought of these pieces. *The Times*, for example, pronounced that '*Rigoletto* has about the same likelihood of maintaining a permanent place on the London Italian stage as its now forgotten predecessor' – this was a reference to *I Masnadieri*, which Verdi had composed for Her Majesty's Theatre and Jenny Lind in 1847.

The fire that destroyed the second Covent Garden broke out at the close of a large fancy dress ball (on the night of 5th March, 1856) organized by a Mr Anderson, known as the 'Wizard of the North'. On the day following the fire the ruins were visited by Queen Victoria, the Prince Consort, and the Princess Royal. The Duke of Bedford, who still owned the freehold of the Covent Garden site, immediately announced his intention of rebuilding the theatre as quickly as possible; and Gye announced that he would continue to give opera at the Lyceum until the new Covent Garden Theatre was ready. His artists rallied to his support, many agreeing to take cuts in their salaries to help him; and Costa also remained loyal to Gye.

The fire had done its work all too well; virtually the whole building and its contents, including the scenery, costumes and properties of sixty operas, were lost. All that was saved were an armful of private documents from Gye's office and, miraculously, Costa's own piano.

THE AGE OF PATTI

But it was all of two years before the third and present Covent Garden Theatre was open to the public; the delay was caused by the time that elapsed between the fire and the signing of the new lease with the Duke of Bedford – a lease that originally was not due to expire until 1947, but which was renewed and later extended until the end of 1949 when the theatre was taken over by the Ministry of Works. Gye chose Edward Barry, son of the designer of the Houses of Parliament and brother of the engineer who designed Tower Bridge, as architect and the foundation stone of the new theatre was laid in October 1857.

The new theatre, unlike its two predecessors, ran east to west rather than north to south; this necessitated purchasing more land to the west of the original site. The remaining land, to the south of the old theatre, was used for the erection of the Floral Hall, a giant Crystal Palace-like Conservatory, which was originally used for concerts and reverted to the Opera House when the market moved away in 1974. The exterior of the present theatre is much higher than its predecessor; and behind the portico, with its five columns of Portland stone, are those Flaxman panels which somehow managed to survive the fire.

White and gold were the colours chosen by Gye for the painted decorations of the auditorium, with warm crimson and rose-coloured hangings providing a contrast. The auditorium of today has changed little since 1858 though the old gallery and amphitheatre have been joined up and made into one large area; no longer do three tiers of private boxes sweep round the house, all subscribed for by 'the nobility and gentry'. Gone too is the great chandelier that hung from the centre of the auditorium, obscuring half the gallery's view and generating an excessive heat. In 1901 it was removed, when all the gas fittings were replaced by electric light. Covent Garden's operatic lore includes the story that when Tamagno, the great Italian tenor, first sang Verdi's *Otello* there in 1895, his ringing top notes were so powerful that the chandelier actually shook, so it was considered prudent to remove the chandelier when he returned to sing the role six years later in case of accidents! Stored away for some time, it was restored and now hangs at the top of the grand staircase just outside the doors leading to the crush-bar. But Queen Victoria's young profile still looks down from above the proscenium arch and the clusters of lights around the auditorium are still supported by cherubs. Anyone who has sniffed the atmosphere of the house will never forget it.

Various structural alterations outside the auditorium have naturally taken place: new staircases and fire-exits; the building of a new wing behind the theatre in 1934 which contained what forty odd years ago were considered 'modern' dressing rooms, but which today are rather spartan; a chorus rehearsal room and storage place for scenery which by post-World War II standards, and compared with the rebuilt opera houses of the continent, have been described as woefully inadequate, or even likened to slum conditions.

So, according to Gye's schedule and the amazement of all concerned, not least himself, seven months after the work had begun the new theatre opened on Saturday, 15th May, 1858, with Meyerbeer's *Les Huguenots* (or *Gli Ugonotti* as it was then called). Grisi, 'as glorious as ever', sang Valentine, and Mario, 'reviving memories of his best days', was Raoul; while the rest of the cast included Nantier–Didiée, Tagliafico, Zegler, and Polonini, with Costa, of course, conducting. Of the 1689 seats only 800 were occupied, the performance was very late in starting and there were long delays in changing the scenery. At nearly 12.30 the curtain fell at the end of the third act – on this occasion after the great Valentine–Raoul scene, act four of the original version – and there was still one whole act left to go. An announcement was then made to the audience from the stage by Harris, the stage manager and father of the more famous Augustus Harris who was to become the director of Covent Garden thirty years later, reminding them of the lateness of the hour, and of the fact that it 'already was the Sabbath Day' and inviting them therefore to join in the singing of God Save the Queen. Contemporary records reveal that 'cat-calls and hisses came from the upper parts of the house, where people baulked of their entertainment became violent, uttering unseemly sounds with which we have never before heard our national anthem accompanied. It was well the Queen was not present!' Nor incidentally was Gye; for he had suffered a nervous collapse, following the stresses of getting his new theatre opened in time.

Although Queen Victoria was not present on the opening night of the new theatre, she and the Prince Consort remained, as they always had been, frequent visitors to Covent Garden. The Queen's constant visits to the opera had resulted in three famous Covent Garden traditions: the National Anthem was never played except on the first and last nights of the season and on State occasions, a dispensation granted because of the necessity hitherto caused by the late arrival of the royal family at the opera to suspend the performance in mid-stream while the audience stood for the anthem. Even Queen Victoria found this disturbing, especially as she was a great opera-lover, and she commanded Gye to let the performance continue without interruption. The second tradition arose as a result of a performance of *Fidelio* which the Queen attended where the Italian choristers, in the guise of soldiers, slouched on to the stage out of time with the music. She sent for Gye and told him: 'Our soldiers can do better than that!' Ever since, troops from the London barracks have been used as extras in those operas demanding large numbers of people to swell the stage processions. Lastly, Her Majesty found the blue lights of Bow Street Police Station, whose entrance faces that of the Opera House, too depressing. So it is the only police station in London not to have blue lights outside it.

After Prince Albert's death in 1861 the Queen was never to set foot in a public place of entertainment again; in the 1880s and 90s, however, singers and musicians from Covent Garden were frequently 'commanded' to perform at both Buckingham Palace and Windsor Castle, and at the latter complete performances of operas were occasionally given.

Grisi's London career had begun in 1834, and in July 1861, the year that Patti made her debut, the two sopranos appeared together in *Don Giovanni*: Grisi as Donna Anna, Patti as Zerlina. In that same year Grisi retired. Patti was her natural successor.

Patti had arrived in London virtually unheralded, having originally been engaged by Mapleson to sing at Her Majesty's. The wily Gye had paid Smith, the lessee of her Majesty's, £4,000 not to proceed with his season; so when Patti arrived in London it was to learn that the season at Her Majesty's was not going to take place after all; she suggested to Mapleson that he himself should finance an opera season, as she was sure that her singing would attract large audiences. Mapleson accordingly took the Lyceum, and went off to the continent to engage a strong company of singers. Meanwhile Patti and her brother-in-law, Maurice Strakosch, who acted as her manager, accurately summed up London's operatic scene and set off to see Gye at Covent Garden to ask for an engagement. Gye, who had probably never heard of Patti, told them his engagements for the season were complete, and that he did not need another soprano. Strakosch, however, suggested that Gye should at least hear her sing, and the Covent Garden manager reluctantly agreed. Hardly had Patti opened her mouth than Gye realised that, for the asking, he could engage a successor to Grisi; this he did by paying Patti an advance of £50 and signing a contract. So when Mapleson returned he was faced with a *fait accompli*.

Patti was originally engaged for Covent Garden for a preliminary period of five years at a salary beginning at £150 a month, and rising by £50 each year so that it reached £400 a month in the fifth year. She was to sing twice a week and was to receive £100 for each performance she might be called on above the agreed two a week. Patti's success was phenomenal and she appeared at Covent Garden every season for the next 25 years, singing more than thirty roles, and ending up as the highest paid singer of her day – at £200 per performance. She was the first London Aida, the first Juliette, and remained unrivalled for the beauty and purity of her tone.

Patti's great popularity can only be compared with that of the pop star of the 1970s. Her every appearance was greeted hysterically; young men waited for her at the stage door, and on one occasion unharnessed the horses from her carriage and dragged it through the streets in a torch-lit procession to her hotel. On 'Patti nights' it was virtually impossible to obtain seats. Like her successors, Albani and Melba, Patti exercised an influence on the management when it came to the choice of repertory and singers. She was extremely jealous of her position, and when she learned that the Swedish soprano, Christine Nilsson, was being paid the same fee (£200 per performance) by Mapleson at Drury Lane, she protested to Gye who agreed to pay her 200 guineas. Pride was satisfied.

Returning to Covent Garden during the Harris regime in 1895 to sing Violetta in La Traviata, Patti wore a magnificent white dress, studded with thirty-seven hundred diamonds worth £200,000. Among the 'guests' in the Party scene were two detectives from Bow Street.

Although such works as *L'Africaine*, *Don Carlos*, *Faust*, *Roméo et Juliette*, *Mignon*, and *Luisa Miller* were added to the Covent Garden repertory during the 1860s and early '70s, Gye relied more and more on the old favourites to fill the house. He virtually ignored Wagner and London lagged far behind the other European capitals in introducing the great German composer's works to its public. *Lohengrin* did not reach London until 1875, nearly a quarter of a century after its first performance, and *Tannhäuser*, which followed in 1876, was nearly thirty-one years later. Both works were sung for many years at Covent Garden in Italian!

Wagner was not the only composer whose works were neglected by Gye; virtually all Verdi's post-*La traviata* operas suffered in the same way. *Don Carlos*, it is true was produced by Gye in 1867, but soon vanished from the repertory; but *Les Vêpres Siciliennes* has never been produced there; while *La forza del destino* was not heard until 1931, and *Simon Boccanegra* only arrived in 1965! *Aida*, probably because it happened to be a 'Patti' opera for its first four seasons, fared rather better.

Gye's regime lasted until 1877 when he was succeeded by his son Ernest, married to the Canadian soprano, Emma Albani. The younger Gye was certainly not as adept as his father in dealing with requests from Patti to mount second- and third-rate operas that had been specially written for her. So after Prince Poniatowski's *Gelmina* and Jules Cohen's *Estella* came Charles Lenepveu's *Velleda*, which was a complete fiasco. The *Sunday Times* critic, Herman Klein, wrote: 'We can only trust that its failure will prove a lesson to Mme Patti not to bring over any more unknown operas by obscure Frenchmen simply because they provide soprano parts well suited to the diva's voice and means.'

It was this kind of nonsense, coupled with higher fees and other conditions imposed by singers like Patti (she insisted on sending her maid to stand in for her at rehearsal, and of having her name on the posters in larger size than anyone else's), that caused inferior supporting artists to be engaged, resulting in a considerable decline in both musical and artistic quality. This lowering of standards was brought home forcibly to the operatic public in 1882 when there were seasons of superbly produced and sung German opera at the two other London theatres at which opera was staged.

Her Majesty's introduced Wagner's *Ring* to England, when three cycles of the great work were given, conducted by Anton Seidl, while Drury Lane held the first performances in England of *Tristan und Isolde* and *Die Meistersinger*, conducted by Hans Richter, who was later to play an important role in establishing Covent Garden's own Wagner tradition. Two years later in 1884, Ernest Gye decided to include twelve performances of German opera in the Covent Garden repertory under Richter with leading Bayreuth singers. Public demand increased these performances to fifteen, but none the less some £2,400 was lost. It now seemed too late to restore the fortunes of Covent Garden, and the younger Gye retired at the end of the season. To quote Klein again: 'The history of the house in the early eighties furnished some melancholy chapters of decaying grandeur, of diminishing artistic effort and public support.'

After Gye's departure, Mapleson returned to Covent Garden in 1885 and 1887; Signor Lago, for many years one of Covent Garden's stage managers, decided to try his hand as an operatic impresario in 1886 and 1887. Although he lowered admission prices and abolished the claque, he failed to win the support of London Society. The claque had long been a bone of contention between singers and managements. This group, engaged by an artist to applaud and demand encores, received free tickets for performances, if not actual money; and the clause 'faveurs de claque' was often inserted in a contract. (True, the Covent Garden claque did not, as was customary in Italy, issue a tariff of charges which ranged from 15 lire for 'insistent applause' to 50 for an encore, and a special sum to be negotiated for 'wild enthusiasm'.)

It was under Mapleson's successor, Augustus Harris, that Covent Garden became one of Europe's most splendid operatic institutions.

A GOLDEN AGE

Augustus Harris was the grandson of Joseph Glossop, who had built the Coburg Hall in the Waterloo Road (later the Old Vic) and for a period was the manager of both the Scala in Milan and the San Carlo in Naples. His father had been Gye's stage manager and had held the same position at the Théâtre des Italiens in Paris where Harris junior was born. Opera, certainly, was in his blood.

Augustus acted for a few years as Mapleson's stage manager, and then, in 1879, with financial help from his father-in-law, Frank Rendle, took over the lease of the Theatre Royal, Drury Lane, a stone's throw from the opera house, where, in 1882, he was instrumental in bringing the German company, already mentioned, to London. In 1887, the year of Queen Victoria's Golden Jubilee, he decided to put on a trial season of Italian opera at Dury Lane, which proved so successful that he was persuaded to take over Covent Garden for the following year.

Augustus planned either 'to give grand opera a decent burial or resuscitate it'. It was resuscitated. Like Gye senior, Harris was able to count on royal patronage; and the Prince and Princess of Wales (later Edward VII and Queen Alexandra) gave society a lead – and were regular visitors to Covent Garden during the fashionable season. Harris had the help and advice of two influential people: Herman Klein, music critic of The *Sunday Times*, who became Harris's 'unofficial' artistic adviser, and Lady de Grey, later the Marchioness of Ripon, a leading figure in London society, who was to exercise an enormous influence both behind and in front of the curtain until 1914. Harris, a sheriff of the City of London and later knighted by Queen Victoria, was wealthy enough to purchase The *Sunday Times* in order to 'protect himself if necessary from unfair adversaries, and if necessary retaliate in kind'. One of Harris's staunchest supporters was Bernard Shaw, who as 'Corno di Bassetto' was writing musical criticism in The *Star*.

Harris's first season brought a prima donna who was to reign at Covent Garden as Patti's successor for the next quarter of a century – the Australian Nellie Melba. During the eight summers from 1889 until his sudden death in 1896, there was a series of unforgettable performances at Covent Garden. Not only did Harris engage the finest singers of the day then active – Melba, Nordica, Calvé, Emma Eames, Jean and Edouard de Reszke, Jean Lassalle, Pol Plançon, De Lucia, and Tamagno – but he also mounted the repertory with a display of great visual opulence which, if not always in the best of taste, delighted the London public. Many new works were heard for the first time in London including *Falstaff*, *Manon Lescaut*, *Werther*, and *Pagliacci*. Wagner at last came into his own at Covent Garden and before very long German opera was being sung in German and French opera in French, instead of everything in an Italian translation. Covent Garden became in fact, as well as in name, the Royal Opera, the word Italian being quietly dropped from its title.

Two other important changes took place during Harris's short regime. The first was the gradual change in the type of

Nellie Melba 1905

*Autographed drawing of the celebrated Australian singer, Nellie Melba,
engaged by Harris in 1888* (Mansell Collection)

audience, especially for Wagner operas, which were especially attractive to the large German-Jewish colony that lived in London, and with which Harris had many contacts through his city connections. The second change was in the auditorium, where Harris introduced electric light and, what was even more revolutionary, he decided, at least for the Wagner performances, to dim them during the performance, instead of leaving them on, as had been the custom hitherto. This decision greatly annoyed that section of the Covent Garden audience that went to the opera house to be seen rather than listen to the performance. The correspondence columns of *The Times* and The *Morning Post* reflected the indignation of London Society as well as of those amateurs who complained that they were unable to read their librettos during the performances.

Harris was well aware that there were, in fact, two different publics for opera in London; those who came to Covent Garden to hear Melba and the de Reszkes, and those who were interested in hearing German opera, sung in the original, and superlatively conducted. In 1892, therefore, he arranged for the principals of the Hamburg Opera, under their musical director the young Gustav Mahler, to come to Covent Garden to give a series of performances of German opera, including the first *Ring* cycle at the theatre.

Harris's sudden death in 1896 did not mean the end of the new 'golden age' at Covent Garden; this continued under the Grand Opera Syndicate with various managers and musical directors. From 1897 to 1900 the Czech impresario, Maurice Grau, who at the time of his appointment was also the sole manager of the Metropolitan Opera in New York, controlled the destinies of both houses. The years 1901 to 1904 saw the French composer André Messager in command; he was also the musical director of the Opéra-Comique in Paris. Messager continued nominally as 'manager' of Covent Garden for another three seasons, during which time there emerged three men, who were to direct the policy of the Royal Opera House for the next decade: the general manager Neil Forsythe, the German conductor Hans Richter, and the English conductor Percy Pitt.

Pitt and Richter formulated a grand plan for presenting permanent opera in English, which was launched by nothing less than giving Wagner's *Ring* in English, in 1907 and 1908, sung by English-speaking singers from England, America, Germany, and Scandinavia. These English *Ring* performances were a huge success financially and artistically, and Pitt and Richter seemed set to proceed with their plans. But the Syndicate, prompted no doubt by Lady de Grey and her committee, killed the scheme by putting every obstacle in the way of Pitt and Richter. Had the excellent work of those two conductors been allowed to continue, it is more than probable that a permanent British national opera company would have been established before the First World War.

The period 1900 to 1914 was, nonetheless, a glorious one for opera at Covent Garden, with the debuts of Caruso, Tetrazzini, Destinn, Martinelli and other great singers of the day. Among the operas that received their first performances in England were *Tosca*, *Madama Butterfly*, *Louise*, *Pelléas et Mélisande*, *La fanciulla del West*, and *Parsifal*; it was a truly golden age of opera.

It has been said, with some truth, that a 'golden age', be it of singing, painting, literature, or indeed of any art form, is always the one before the present, and the one that we heard about from our parents and grandparents. There is no valid reason why the so-called 'golden age' at Covent Garden before the First World War was any more of a golden age than that of the mid-19th century, or the time of the Wagner performances in the 1920s and '30s. Perhaps there is a kind of nostalgia for the kind of social life that existed in London in the Edwardian period and in the first years of King George V's reign which causes historians, both social and political, to see those years through rose-tinted spectacles. Indeed, the magnificent Royal Gala performances at Covent Garden from 1903 to 1914, whether they were for the King of Spain, the King of Denmark or the President of France, when single acts from the popular operas were given with the greatest singers of the day in the casts, all contribute to our picture of a golden age. On these occasions the programmes were printed on rich white silk bearing portraits of the royal family and their guests, and the scale of decorations in the Royal Box and the auditorium were of a splendour which today would be considered excessive and astonishingly extravagant.

Not all these performances reflected a calm and contented society. At the 1911 Coronation Gala, when the auditorium was decorated with 100,000 rose blooms, the scent of which caused many ladies to faint, the programme was made up of excerpts from French and Italian opera and Russian ballet. At the instigation of the Kaiser, the German Press protested. The 1914 Royal Gala for the King and Queen of Denmark was interrupted just before the Triumph scene from *Aida* was due to commence by a suffragette demonstration; leaflets were showered on the audience.

All these events took place during the so-called 'grand season', which lasted from May to the end of July; but shorter seasons were often given in spring and autumn, and it was during these that a new figure emerged. A man who was to play a leading role in British operatic life during the next quarter of a century: Thomas Beecham. In the three seasons he gave at Covent Garden, which were financed by his father Sir Joseph Beecham on the profits made from patent medicines, he gave the first performances in England of Strauss's *Elektra*, *Salome*, and *Der Rosenkavalier*, and such novelties as Delius's *A Village Romeo and Juliet* and Ethel Smyth's *The Wreckers*. Beecham's autobiography, *A Mingled Chime*, gives a highly amusing account of his clashes with the censor over *Salome* and *Der Rosenkavalier*. He quotes with relish the decision arrived at in the last act of *Rosenkavalier*: the bed could be sung about with the 'offensive' words removed so long as it remained hidden from the audience – 'a nearly perfect sample of our British love of compromise'.

Beecham was passionately dedicated to opera, and rumours abounded that he had come to an agreement with the Metropolitan Opera in New York to present a season at Drury Lane for the summer of 1911, King George V's coronation year. A

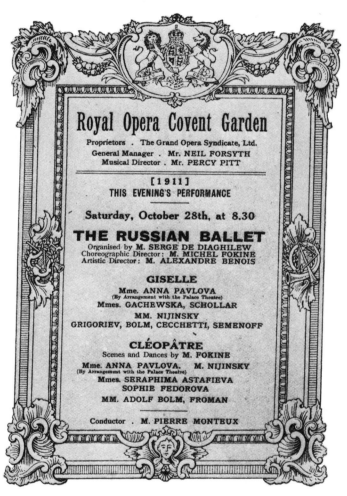

Royal Opera Covent Garden

Proprietors . The Grand Opera Syndicate, Ltd.
General Manager . Mr. NEIL FORSYTH
Musical Director . Mr. PERCY PITT

[1911]
THIS EVENING'S PERFORMANCE

Saturday, October 28th, at 8.30

THE RUSSIAN BALLET

Organised by M. SERGE DE DIAGHILEW
Choreographic Director: M. MICHEL FOKINE
Artistic Director: M. ALEXANDRE BENOIS

GISELLE

Mme. ANNA PAVLOVA
(By Arrangement with the Palace Theatre)
Mmes. GACHEWSKA, SCHOLLAR

MM. NIJINSKY
GRIGORIEV, BOLM, CECCHETTI, SEMENOFF

CLÉOPÂTRE

Scenes and Dances by M. FOKINE

Mme. ANNA PAVLOVA.   M. NIJINSKY
(By Arrangement with the Palace Theatre)
Mmes. SERAPHIMA ASTAFIEVA
SOPHIE FEDOROVA

MM. ADOLF BOLM, FROMAN

Conductor . M. PIERRE MONTEUX

*Famous names from the Russian Ballet Company which first performed
at Covent Garden in 1911 (Victoria and Albert Museum)*

repertory of twenty operas was announced with Toscanini as joint conductor with Beecham. In addition, Diaghilev's Russian Ballet company had been engaged for a series of performances. This potential rivalry was too much for Covent Garden, and the Grand Opera Syndicate decided to invite Beecham to join their board. Beecham accepted on condition that his agreement with the Russian Ballet Company was taken over by Covent Garden; and the Syndicate in turn suggested that the recently formed Beecham Symphony Orchestra should occupy the pit at Covent Garden on ballet nights. And so Russian ballet came to London, and the foundations of Covent Garden's ballet traditions were laid.

IN LIVING MEMORY

The theatre was closed during the First World War and was requisitioned by the government as a furniture repository – an indignity only surpassed during the Second World War, when it was turned into a *palais de dance*. When Covent Garden re-opened in May 1919, it was with Beecham as artistic director, the first in the history of the Opera House. As a result of various financial dealings during the war, Beecham and his father had become involved in specific transactions bringing them into possession of the Covent Garden estate which included The Royal Opera House, the Theatre Royal, Drury Lane, and the whole market area. As Beecham himself said, the possession of the Opera House was 'more honourable than profitable, for the Grand Opera Syndicate had an old lease on the building which still had twenty years to run, for which they paid the modest sum of 750 pounds a year!'

During that first post-war season the most interesting Covent Garden debut, at least in retrospect, was made by a young Irish ballerina who had become the principal dancer of the Beecham Opera Company: her name was Ninette de Valois, and she danced in *Aida*, *Louise*, and *Samson et Dalila*, little thinking that after the Second World War Covent Garden would become the home of a still undreamed-of British national ballet company.

In 1920 Beecham found himself in financial difficulties, and did not conduct opera there again until 1932. His opera company refused to be disbanded, and formed itself into the British National Opera Company, occupying Covent Garden for winter and summer seasons between 1922 and 1924 and touring the country for the rest of the year. Once again it looked as if permanent British opera was to become established. And once again, as with the Pitt-Richter *Ring*, it was the Syndicate that dealt a death blow to native opera when in 1924, the year of the British Empire Exhibition at Wembley, it denied the use of the theatre to the company, deciding instead to return to international opera.

From 1924 to 1931, Bruno Walter and German opera prospered at Covent Garden. This was the period of Frida Leider, Lotte Lehmann, Elisabeth Schumann, Maria Olczewska, Lauritz Melchior, Friedrich Schorr, Herbert Janssen, Ivar Andrésen, and Richard Mayr; the years of the brilliant *Rosenkavalier* performances and the infectious production of Johann Strauss's *Die Fledermaus*, which was making its first appearance at Covent Garden. Italian opera fared less well, though there were some memorable performances with Rosa Ponselle, Rosetta Pampanini, Gigli, Pertile, Pinza, and Stabile. Those summer performances occupied the theatre for only about eight or ten weeks each summer; for the rest of the time Covent Garden was used as a dance hall.

In 1931 the Socialist government, with Snowden as Chancellor of the Exchequer, granted the first small public subsidy to Covent Garden; it was £15,000 a year and paid to the theatre through the BBC – a fraction of its licence money. A link with Downing Street was provided by inviting Lady Snowden to join the board of directors; she was an assiduous letter writer, and bombarded Colonel Eustace Blois, the theatre's managing director, with almosy daily communications, urging the production of this or that opera by British composers. In 1931 the great depression hit Great Britain, and it seemed highly unlikely that there would be any more opera at Covent Garden. Then in 1932 Beecham was persuaded to return, and he conducted a four-week season of Wagner opera. From 1933 to 1939 he directed the destinies of the opera house.

Those were the years of the famous Rossini performances with Conchita Supervia; of Mozart under Beecham with Richard Tauber, Erna Berger, Elisabeth Rethberg and Pinza; the great Wagner evenings with Kirsten Flagstad, Ludwig Weber, Alexander Kipnis and others, with either Beecham, Furt-wängler, Fritz Reiner, or Weingartner at the conductor's desk. In 1936 came the controversial visit of the Dresden State Opera when Strauss himself conducted his *Ariadne auf Naxos*; controversial because of the anti-Nazi feeling of the day, and because Ribbentrop, the German Ambassador in London, appeared in the Royal Box and gave the Nazi salute.

If there were uncomfortable political undertones to the Dresden State Opera's visit, artistically it gave rise to serious thought about the visual side of opera at Covent Garden. With the exception of the settings for the 1934 *Fidelio* by Rex Whistler, the new look for the *Ring* the same year and the Rossini operas for Conchita Supervia, Covent Garden productions were visually almost a quarter of a century behind the times. And so the Dresden Company's visit, with its integrated performances, fine ensemble and attractive visual aspect, made a profound impression. This, coupled with what was going on at John Christie's new Glyndebourne Opera, which had opened in 1934 under the direction of Fritz Busch and Carl Ebert, clearly showed that opera was something more than just singing, and that production and unity of style were elements just as important in the perfect operatic performance.

Ballet, too, gained a foothold at this time. Ida Rubinstein's company appeared there in 1931; the Camargo Society gave two gala evenings in 1933; and from 1934 to 1939 De Basil's Company, under various names, gave yearly seasons. Most prophetically of all, however, on 22nd May, 1939, the Vic-Wells Ballet appeared for the first time in the Opera House at the Gala

Performance for the French President. Margot Fonteyn danced, as she was so often to do in the post-war period; she was seen as Princess Aurora in Acts 1 and 3 of the *Sleeping Princess*, as it was then announced. In between the two acts, Sir Thomas Beecham conducted the London Philharmonic in a performance of Debussy's *Iberia*; 'the orchestra was superb,' wrote a leading critic, 'but it was depressing and obscure for the occasion. Any chance of the Cabinet ever subsidising symphonic music was killed dead last night.' Fortunately a false prophecy, for when Covent Garden began operations after the Second World War, the prospect of subsidy for the arts had become a reality.

COVENT GARDEN TODAY

✸

It was in 1945 that the Covent Garden Opera Trust, under the chairmanship of the late Lord Keynes, decided that post-war Covent Garden should become the national home of opera and ballet, operating the whole year round. The theatre had been saved from a further period of being used as a dance hall by the prompt action taken by the music publishers, Boosey and Hawkes, who in 1945 secured a short lease of the property which ran until the end of 1949. In that year, as many people hoped, the Ministry of Works negotiated a forty-two years' lease with the ground landlords, Covent Garden Properties Ltd., and then sublet the theatre to the Royal Opera House, Covent Garden Limited, which received from the Arts Council an annual subsidy; a strange situation, with the government in theory paying itself rent for a national opera house! For its ballet company the Trust did not have far to look, and by agreement with the governors of Sadler's Wells, the Sadler's Wells Ballet with Dame Ninette de Valois, Constant Lambert and Frederick Ashton as its guiding lights was transferred to the Opera House and became its resident company; eventually, in 1956, it was granted a charter of incorporation from the Queen, and became known as the Royal Ballet.

And so it was with ballet that the Royal Opera House reopened its doors on the 20th February 1946 with a performance of *The Sleeping Beauty*, in the beautiful settings designed by Oliver Messel; this time it was given in its entirety, with Margot Fonteyn and Robert Helpmann. The Royal Box was occupied by King George VI, Queen Elizabeth, Queen Mary, and the Princesses, Elizabeth and Margaret.

For opera there was no such easy solution, and a company had to be built up from scratch. To this end the Trust appointed as musical director Karl Rankl, an Austrian refugee. A former pupil of Schoenberg and Webern, he became Klemperer's assistant in Berlin, and afterwards musical director of the Graz Opera until the Nazi occupation, when he moved to the German Opera in Prague until 1939. The infant Covent Garden Opera Company began life in December 1946 by joining with the Ballet in a series of performances of Purcell's *The Fairy Queen* until, on 14th January, 1947, it appeared on its own in a performance of *Carmen*.

During the post-war period the Opera Company has had four musical directors: Karl Rankl from 1946 to 1951; Rafael Kubelik from 1955 to 1959; Sir Georg Solti from 1961 to 1971; and Colin Davis since 1971; and for the first twenty-four years, presiding over all the activities of the Opera House was the figure of Sir David Webster. But for him Covent Garden would surely have had to cease its activities. During the two difficult periods when the Opera Company had no musical director, it was largely due to his patience and common sense that it achieved such successes as *Wozzeck* conducted by Erich Kleiber, and the series of Wagner and Strauss performances conducted by Rudolf Kempe; it was David Webster, too, who succeeded in luring the great Otto Klemperer back to opera and in engaging Carlo Maria Giulini to conduct Verdi for several seasons.

If Rankl was responsible for building up the infant company and laying the foundations upon which all the others were to build, it was Kleiber and Kempe who first gave British singers the chances to appear abroad and gave them confidence. It was Kubelik who believed in the company spirit and ensemble opera, and his short period as musical director was climaxed by the first full stage production of Berlioz's *The Trojans*, with only one guest artist. It was Solti who brought glamour and excitement to the house, and raised the standards of orchestral playing to great heights; and it has been Colin Davis, together with John Tooley, David Webster's successor, who have sought to bring a new image to Covent Garden, to rejuvenate it and widen its audience. All these great personalities have contributed to raising the international standard of Covent Garden. While it was comparatively easy for the Royal Ballet to win acclaim in Europe and America, it was far more difficult for British singers to do so. Nonetheless, the acceptance on equal terms with their continental colleagues of such artists as Joan Sutherland, Amy Shuard, Josephine Veasey, Gwyneth Jones, Jon Vickers, Geraint Evans, Donald McIntyre, and David Ward, to mention just a few names, has proved just how quickly Covent Garden's operatic tradition has been established. In October 1968, the Covent Garden Opera, like its sister ballet company, was honoured by the Queen and became known as the Royal Opera – at last the company – not the building – was being honoured. Two years later Solti was able to take the Royal Opera on a successful visit to Munich and Berlin; and in the spring of 1976 it is paying its first visit to La Scala in Milan.

Everyone will have his or her special memories of the outstanding events at Covent Garden over the last quarter of a century or more: the Fonteyn and Nureyev nights; the splendid Ashton ballets; the emergence of a new generation of young dancers like Anthony Dowell and Antoinette Sibley, Lynn Seymour and Donald MacLeary; the visits to the theatre by the Bolshoi and Kirov companies which no balletomane will ever forget. For the opera fan there have been Flagstad, Birgit Nilsson, and Hans Hotter in Wagner; the Callas-Gobbi *Tosca*, and indeed many other operas in which both these great artists appeared on the London stage; the Peter Hall-Solti *Moses and Aaron*; *Pelléas et Mélisande* conducted by Boulez; the now legendary *Don Carlos* conducted by Giulini for the present theatre's centenary in 1958; the Klemperer *Fidelio*; and more recently Colin Davis conducting Mozart's *La clemenza di Tito* with Janet Baker. And there were the Royal Galas, which today are unique in the world's opera houses.

But audiences themselves indeed change, and one wonders what Melba would have made of the annual Covent Garden 'proms', when the stalls are all taken up and the space is filled with young people, informally dressed, seeing and hearing the best in opera and ballet for the modest price of 50 pence.

It would be foolish to try to prophecy whether the Royal Opera and Royal Ballet will be functioning in the 1980s as they are today; and to assume that the exciting schemes for the development of the Market Area, which include extensions to the Opera House and the building of suitable premises to house the Royal Ballet School and the London Opera Centre, to say nothing of the building of a smaller auditorium, will ever be realised. One hopes that they will. Meanwhile, as long as the two resident companies occupy the famous theatre they will surely continue not only to build up the traditions of Covent Garden, but also to add to its memories, so that future writers can expand this brief chronicle.

ACKNOWLEDGEMENTS

The colour plates appear by courtesy of the following people, collections and organisations: 1, 15, Covent Garden Archive; 2, Tate Gallery; 3, Museum of London; 4, 12, Mansell Collection; 5, 6, 7, 9, 11, Trustees of the British Museum; 8, 10, Victoria and Albert Museum; 13, Fine Art Society; 14, Frank Sharman, FRPS; 16, A. F. Kersting.

*1. Gala programme designed by Rex Whistler for the Royal Command
Performance in honour of the French President, March 1939*

2. *A Scene from the* Beggar's Opera *by William Hogarth, 1729. It was this production which made John Rich rich enough to build Covent Garden Theatre.*

3. *Covent Garden Piazza and Market by John Collet, c. 1770–80*

4. *Tom and Jerry in the Saloon at Covent Garden, drawn and engraved by I. R. and G. Cruikshank*

5. Cruikshank's view of the O.P. riots

6. *Interior of the first theatre, 1808, showing Handel's organ: from Ackermann's 'Microcosm of London', drawn and engraved by Pugin and Rowlandson*

7. *The entrance to the pit of the first theatre, from Bow Street:*
watercolour by T. H. Shepherd

8. *Angelica Catalani
in 1824, on her
return to England in
'Il fanatico':
Watercolour by
A. E. Chalon*

9. Madame Adelina Patti as Esmeralda: music cover lithograph

10. *East front of the second theatre, designed by Robert Smirke, showing the Flaxman*

11. *The second theatre burning, masquerades in the streets, on 5th March, 1856:*
coloured lithograph

12. Spy cartoon of Augustus Harris, from Vanity Fair.

13. *Design by Léon Bakst for a costume for 'Narcisse', one of the Diaghilev ballets produced in London in 1911*

14 'The Sleeping Beauty' designed by Oliver Messel and starring Margot Fonteyn · colour

15. *Design by Hainer Hill for Acts I and II of 'Lohengrin', 1963*

16. The interior of Covent Garden today